Copyright © 2021 by Nima Shiningstar-EL

Published by Sunshine BlackRose PublicationsSouth Carolina, USA www.SunshineBRPublications.com

All rights reserved. Printed in the United States of America. No part of this book may be used or reproduced, stored in a retrieval system, or transmitted in any manner whatsoever without written permission. The only exception is brief quotations in printed reviews.

Cover design by Sunshine BlackRose Publications

ISBN: 978-1732191068

The Year was 2008.

It was the year the Philadelphia Phillies won the World Series. It was the year that We put President Barak Obama in office. Something even more spectacular happened that year...

Jawhara Nima Williams was born. GOD blessed us with you and this family is forever grateful.

You are smart, funny, and very artistic. Your paintings and stories are fantastic. Continue to grow and learn. You can be anything you set your mind and abilities to. You are beautiful inside and out.

Remember to treat people with kindness and make sure they treat you the same way.

I love you very much...Grandmom

"Today is a great day to go to the zoo," Jawhara thought to herself. It was summertime and the sun was shining bright. She wondered if her mom and dad had plans once they got home from work.

"Grandma, do you think my mommy and daddy would take me to the zoo if I asked them?"

"It's possible sweetheart, but just in case, have a backup plan," said Grandma.

Jawhara sat a the kitchen table thinking of a backup plan.

Jawhara couldn't think of anything else. She loved the Philadelphia Zoo. It was the best zoo in the world! She loved seeing all the animals and meeting new friends every time she went. In her mind she imagined the beautiful white polar bears and how they swam in the water and looked as if they were having so much fun. Jawhara pretended that she was a polar bear.

"Look Grandma, I'm a polar bear. Are you afraid?"

Grandma said, "I'm not afraid, but I will be careful," with a smile.

Next Jawhara imagined the elephants. She walked very slowly to the living room. She used her arm and hung it low over her nose as she swayed her body to show how elephants move.

"I am an elephant now, "she said.
Jawhara loved to play pretend.

Whenever her mommy and daddy took her to the zoo they sat in the food court and had lunch. Jawhara always had ice cream for dessert.

When Jawhara's mother and father came in the door she immediately ran to them. "Mom, dad can we go to the zoo today!" she said with such excitement. They turned to one another then turned to Grandma."Well, I am a little tired but it's so beautiful outside, I would hate to waste the rest of this day. Hmmm, why not." said her grandma.

Jawhara was so happy she ran full steam to her Pop Pop and told him that they were going to the zoo. They all put on some comfortable clothes, packed some snacks, and water for the trip. The zoo was onlya 10-minute drive from their home which made it easy for Jawhara to get everyone to agree. When they arrived at the zoo there was a very long line. People from all over were coming to see the animals! The line was getting shorter and Jawhara couldn't wait to get inside!

They saw the lions walking back and forth behind the gates. They looked beautiful but they also looked mean. The cubs were playing and te mommy and daddy lion were watching all the people that were watching them.

They went inside to see the snakes. Jawhara did not like the snakes at all. She thought they were too slippery and slimy. She also thought that they could easily sneak up on you. There was one thing she liked and that was the beautiful colors. Some of them had red spots, some were green. Some snakes were black, and others were yellow. Some could swallow you whole and had huge fangs to bite you and give you a deadly dose of venom.
Jawhara was happy the snakes were behind glass.

While the family had lunch Jawhara asked Pop Pop, "What are we going to see next?'

"We can go feed the ducks and watch the peacocks walk around" he said.

Jawhara even made up a song about the peacocks.

♪♫One peacock, two peacock. I see red and blue peacocks. Pretty colors all around. My skin is a beautiful brown. Beautiful feathers in the air. I have braids in my hair. ♫♪

Grandma told Jawhara how she used to love going to the zoo. "Everything was so much cheaper then," she said

Jawhara laughed because every time her grandma told her a story from her childhood, she reminded her how things were so much cheaper back then. She loved her conversations with her grandma.

After they visited the peacocks, the family went to visit the flamingos. The flamingos were so pretty. They looked graceful. They talked to each other while the visitors at the zoo took pictures. "I wonder what they are saying to one another," said Jawhara.

Grandma looked at her and laughed. "They are probably sick of us looking at them." They both laughed.

It was time to go home. Jawhara was talking nonstop all the way home about everything she saw that day. She told her parents and grandparents thank you for taking her to the zoo. They all smiled and asked her what her favorite thing about the zoo was. Jawhara played with her beads and braids and then said with her with a proud voice, "Family, I looked at all the animals that were by themselves and they seemed so sad. They didn't want to play or eat. The ones who had family were having fun playing, jumping, and talking in animal talk. So, I realized that family is super dooper dooper important. We are a family and that's important."